TABLE OF CONTENTS

CHAPTER 1: INTRODUCTION

Since 9/11, the U.S. Government has aggressively pursued Al Qaeda and its agents across the globe. U.S. media headlines have continually covered the U.S. campaign against Al Qaeda and unsurprisingly, Al Qaeda has captured the attention of the U.S. public. In the twelve years since 9/11, the terror concern has focused upon Al Qaeda with the current U.S. National Security Strategy for Counterterrorism dedicating the vast majority of its prose to discussion of the threat provided by Al Qaeda and its affiliates.[1]

While the U.S. Counterterrorism Strategy focuses upon Al Qaeda, the Iranian backed Shi'ite terror group Hezbollah has quietly diversified and improved its capability into a wide spectrum of legal and illicit activities that give it a unique position in the world. The classification of Hezbollah as simply a terror group does not capture its vast and diverse capability and capacity. It is both well-funded and highly capable, largely due to its strong affiliation with the Iranian Revolutionary Guard's Qods Force. Hezbollah's elements of power consist of significant battlefield capability, an established political entity within Lebanon, significant social outreach, highly developed media and information arm, and transnational illicit trafficking. Once a high-profile terror concern of the U.S., Hezbollah has been somewhat less visible since 9/11 as U.S. focus has turned to Al Qaeda. As testament to this reduced visibility, the National Counterterrorism

---

[1] Al Qaeda Arabian Peninsula, Al-Shabaab, Al Qaeda Iraq, Al Qaeda Islamic Maghreb, among others.

Strategy[2] mentions "Hizballah" only twice while mentioning "al-Qa'ida" dozens of times.

Alongside terrorism, problems associated with illegal entry into the U.S. from Mexico have been frequent points of discussion. This discussion's loudest voice centers upon illegal immigration, but other elements, such as drugs and the wider impact of human trafficking (such as the sex trade), are also prevalent. At the center of these illicit transit concerns are Transnational Organized Crime[3] (TOC) groups, such as the Mexican Gulf, Los Zetas and Sinaloa cartels, and the Salvadorian gangs Mara Salvatrucha 13 (MS-13) and *Calle* 18 (18th Street).

Like Hezbollah, TOC groups in Latin America have developed into formidable entities, capable of challenging local, and at times, national governments. Mexican cartels have become wealthy and powerful through the movement of drugs and people (primarily) through transit routes from Mexico into the United States. Similarly, the notorious gangs MS-13 and *Calle* 18 have also grown in power and wealth through illicit trafficking, largely emanating from El Salvador.

Although terror groups, cartels, and gangs garner significant concern by themselves, they pose an even greater concern when they work together. There are strong indications that terror groups and TOCs have already found common purpose in

---

[2] National Security Council, *National Counterterrorism Strategy*, (Washington D.C.: The White House, 2011).

[3] Transnational organized crime refers to those self-perpetuating associations of individuals who operate transnationally for the purpose of obtaining power, influence, monetary and/or commercial gains, wholly or in part by illegal means, while protecting their activities through a pattern of corruption and/ or violence, or while protecting their illegal activities through a transnational organizational structure and the exploitation of transnational commerce or communication mechanisms. There is no single structure under which transnational organized criminals operate; they vary from hierarchies to clans, networks, and cells, and may evolve to other structures. The crimes they commit also vary.
Please see: *NSC*. http://www.whitehouse.gov/administration/eop/nsc/transnational-crime/definition (accessed January 22, 2014).

which to operate and collaborate. "In 2010, 29 of the 63 top drug trafficking organizations identified by the Department of Justice had links to terrorist organizations."[4] Although concerning, a nexus of terror groups and TOCs is not a new phenomenon, "The failure of the international community to recognize the centrality of this unholy trinity allowed this nexus to flourish in the 1990s and the beginning of this century."[5]

Interaction between Hezbollah and TOCs produces a grave synergy; "This emerging combination of threats comprises a hybrid of criminal-terrorist, and state and non-state franchises, combining multiple nations acting in concert, and traditional TOCs and terrorist groups acting as proxies for the nation states that sponsor them."[6] Address of this complex threat will require a detailed and comprehensive solution that spans a wide range of capabilities, "Understanding and mitigating the threat requires a whole-of-government approach, including collection, analysis, law enforcement, policy and programming."[7] This comprehensive approach to dealing with the criminal-terror nexus will require adaptive thought and action as a Westphalian approach will not encompass the totality of dynamics necessary. "No longer is the state/nonstate dichotomy useful in illustrating these problems, just as the TOC/terrorism divide is increasingly disappearing."[8] All of these elements taken together identify this new threat as one that requires new perspectives and discussion, "...the new combination of TOC, criminalized

---

[4] Douglas Farah, "Central America's Northern Triangle: A Time for turmoil and Transitions." *Prism* 4, no. 3 (2013): 88-109.

[5] Louise Shelley, "The Unholy Trinity: Transnational Crime, Corruption, and Terrorism." *Brown Journal of World Affairs* XI, no. 2 (Winter/Spring 2005): 101-111.

[6] Douglass Farah, *Transnational Organized Crime, Terrorism, and Criminalized States in Latin America: An Emerging Tier-One National Security Priority.* (Carlisle Barracks, PA: U.S. Army War College Strategic Studies Institute, 2012): 83.

[7] *Ibid.*, 2.

[8] *Ibid.*, 2.

states, and terrorist organizations presents a new reality that breaks the traditional paradigms."[9]

The anti-American intent and killing capacity of terror groups coupled with the advantageous location, transportation capability, and malign purpose of cartels and gangs presents a real and viable security threat to the United States. With the prospect of a nexus between Hezbollah and the TOCs of Central America, the United States must develop and implement a comprehensive, multi-agency, and international approach to defeat this high priority security threat. Additionally, this approach will need to recognize that Westphalian state-centric concepts are largely ineffective in dealing with this concern. Further, removing their key enabler—their ability to establish operating bases through exploitation of ungoverned spaces and the populations within them—is the crucial point for lasting success. The focus upon lasting success goes beyond Hezbollah and TOCs. The effective models and techniques being employed by these groups should not be viewed as isolated occurrences. Indeed, there is every reason to believe that other illicit organizations will emulate and adapt these models for their own purposes. Thus, an approach that addresses the root causes of current threats presented by today's illicit non-state groups could serve as a model for degrading and defeating similar threats in the future.

Accordingly, the scope of this paper is to introduce an approach to the identified problem, using the specific case example of the nexus between Hezbollah and TOCs. Taking a strategic view would raise the level of national discussion and preclude

---

[9] *Ibid.,* 20.

discussion of the nuances and requirements of operational activities and the interactions of elements at that level.

This paper will address the issue in four primary parts:

1) The threat presented by Hezbollah and TOCs,

2) The nexus between Hezbollah and TOCs, and the key role played by ungoverned spaces,

3) Current U.S. Government activities targeted against these illicit groups and,

4) A proposed national approach to combat this emergent threat, which targets these groups through an integrated tier structure with focus upon the root causes of the concerns.

CHAPTER 2: THE THREAT

The threat presented by the nexus of terror organizations and criminal cartels and gangs presents in a variety of ways. Most of these manifestations are readily recognizable, yet their implications and attendant challenges are complex in nature. There are two basic elements of this threat; terror groups themselves and the TOCs with which they associate. Hezbollah, although not the terror organization *du jour* of the media, has quietly developed into a well-organized, multi-faceted, and global organization.

Hezbollah

The 23 October 1983 bombing of the Marine barracks in Lebanon introduced most of the world to a new terror organization, Hezbollah.[1] While generally considered Hezbollah's most spectacular attack, it is not representative of what this terror organization has become. Indeed, Hezbollah has evolved into a much more formidable and dangerous, multi-faceted organization while maintaining centrality of purpose as identified in its, "…release in 1985 of a manifesto denouncing the 'aggression and humiliation' inflicted by 'America and its allies and the Zionist entity.'"[2]

Once defined simply as a terror organization, Hezbollah now defies definition. Beyond its highly evolved combat and terror capabilities, Hezbollah, under the leadership of Hassan Nasrallah, has also become a highly effective political, media, social, and

---

[1] The organization initially referred to itself as "Islamic Jihad" although it would become known as Hezbollah. Note that there are alternate spellings of "Hezbollah," which will be seen throughout this paper in source quotations, which will be kept intact.
[2] Max Boot, *Invisible Armies: An Epic History of Guerrilla Warfare from Ancient Times to the Present* (New York: Liveright Publishing Corporation, 2013), 750.

criminal organization that enjoys solid popular support in Lebanon, with strong ties to Iran and transnational organized crime organizations. Hezbollah has evolved into a global organization with a wide array of capabilities that have made it significantly more powerful while providing substantial operational reach and flexibility.

In its early actions, suicide bombing was a primary technique for achieving its objectives.[3] Hezbollah eventually discarded these tactics due to a greater understanding of immediate and second order effects. "Indeed, as of 2011, Hezbollah had not mounted a single suicide operation since 1999."[4] This tactical shift indicates recognition that attacks resulting in indiscriminate killing have a negative impact on perceptions of the organization. Nasrallah and his deputies recognized that Hezbollah could have greater impact by avoiding *indiscriminate* violence while manipulating political, social and media mechanisms.

Hezbollah developed and maintains these diverse capabilities through an advanced organizational model, designed to operate remotely while supporting the center:

> A local Hezbollah network usually includes the following components: *Dawa* and recruitment entity, based on religious clerics, Islamic centers, Internet sites, and the broadcasts of Almanar Television; a financing department whose capabilities are based on the ability to raise money legally and illegally by using organized crime; and an operational team, dealing with smuggling activists and means of warfare and the assembling of intelligence concerning potential targets.[5]

Hezbollah has moved far beyond the "simple" construct of a terrorist organization. While there is no question that Hezbollah maintains its extremist roots, it has evolved

---

[3] Even if the actions were contrary to the teachings of the Koran, "Hezbollah brought the... ethos of martyrdom to its operations, even though the Koran expressly forbids the killing of innocents." Boot, *Invisible Armies*, 505.

[4] Boot, *Invisible Armies*, 530.

[5] Eitan Azani, *Hezbollah: The Story of the party of God.* (New York: Palgrave MacMillan, 2009), 204.

beyond what most people consider a terrorist organization to be. In his book, *Invisible Armies*, author Max Hastings refers to Hezbollah as the "A Team" of terror organizations due to its highly evolved organization and capabilities. Indeed, as Hezbollah has developed over the past 20-30 years it has become much more competent, effective, and dangerous. Nowhere was this more evident than in southern Lebanon in 2006.

In 2006, Hezbollah triggered an Israeli invasion of Lebanon by ambushing an Israeli military patrol in northern Israel and capturing two Israeli soldiers. As the Israelis advanced into southern Lebanon, they encountered a highly dedicated and well-trained Hezbollah militia. The capability and ability of the Hezbollah defense shocked all but the Hezbollah fighters themselves. "Hizballah's tactical success surprised most in Israel and many elsewhere. It did not surprise members of the group itself who had spent years preparing southern Lebanon for defense and training to fight on the rugged terrain."[6]

As the world watched the Israeli military fight this surprisingly capable foe, Hezbollah's newly established informational and political capabilities complimented, and in many ways exceeded, their newfound combat prowess. The political and informational wings of Hezbollah turned the tide of the conflict against the Israeli's.

By assuming a strong political position within Lebanon (owning approximately 10% of seats in the national legislature), Hezbollah established a position of national and international legitimacy which gave it a position of strength in both domestic and international settings. This created a new dynamic for Israeli forces to deal with, while providing Hezbollah a pulpit from which to wage an information campaign. This was not a position attained by accident, but through perceptive understanding and calculation.

---

[6] Russell W. Glenn, *All Glory is Fleeting* (Santa Monica, CA: RAND Corporation, 2012), 6.

Nasrallah moved Hezbollah away from being purely a terrorist organization. Like Mao, Ho and Castro, he recognized the importance of political action. Unlike them, he was even willing to compete in more or less free elections, although Nasrallah continued to use considerable coercion to turn out the vote and to silence critics. Over the objections of some members, Hezbollah became a political party that, starting in 1992, competed in Lebanon's elections and appointed cabinet ministers.[7]

The critical element of this political climb was garnering local popular support in Lebanon. Hezbollah's appreciation of the worldview is second only to its understanding of the requirement for a strong base of support—the Shia population in Lebanon. To establish this support base, Hezbollah has assumed the role of societal benefactor through the establishment of a wide variety of humanitarian and licit organizations designed to provide for large portions of the Lebanese population. "Hezbollah has created an impressive social base by setting up an array of public services, including schools, mosques, clinics, hospitals, community centers, and public assistance facilities…This kinder, gentler side of Hezbollah has been used to bolster the party's membership and to increase popular support."[8] Hezbollah has continued to make use of social action to great effect in furthering its political control within Lebanon. In the wake of the 2006 Israeli invasion, "Hezbollah also spent hundreds of millions of dollars to rebuild war-damaged areas, thus strengthening its hold on the Shiite population. In 2011 Hezbollah and its allies toppled Lebanon's Sunni, pro-Western prime minister, Saad Hariri, and replaced him with a politician more to their liking."[9]

Along with Hezbollah's political aspirations has come a heightened appreciation for the impact of perceptions. Not content to rely upon external media to carry, and

---

[7] Boot, *Invisible Armies*, 508.
[8] Avi Jorisch, *Beacon of Hatred: Inside Hizballah's Al-Manar Television* (Washington D.C.: Washington Institue for Near East Policy, 2004), 11.
[9] Boot, *Invisible Armies*, 512.

control, its message, Hezbollah developed its own robust information distribution capability, "… it set up its own website, four newspapers, five radio stations, and a satellite television station, Al Manar (The Lighthouse), to get its message out."[10] Further, Hezbollah also realized the offensive power of media. Just as Hezbollah fighters were demonstrating surprising tactical skill in 2006, combat prowess proved secondary to the strategic effect of information operations. "Where Hezbollah really excelled, however, was not in ground combat but in manipulation of the news media."[11] As Israeli jets destroyed Hezbollah's critical infrastructure, Hezbollah effectively turned tactical losses into strategic victory through allegations of civilian casualties. "Hezbollah had mastered jujitsu information operations, turning its enemy's strength into a disadvantage in the battle for global sympathy."[12]

Demonstrating even greater understanding of the power of information, Hezbollah has become acutely aware of how global perceptions can influence organizational success, "As a pragmatic terrorist organization, Hezbollah is conscious that many of its actions are condemnable to the international community, if exposed."[13] Considering this, Hezbollah countered and then capitalized on this dynamic to "control the narrative," while also clouding its true malign intent to the people of Lebanon and the world. "Nasrallah uses a 'double-faced' policy…to blur the identity of the organization as a terrorist organization and to emphasize the identity of the organization as a political party inside Lebanon and social party inside Lebanon."[14] This deception effort has been

---

[10] *Ibid.*, 508.
[11] *Ibid.*, 511.
[12] *Ibid.*, 512.
[13] Cyrus Miryekta, "Hezbollah in the Tri-Border Area of South America." *smallwarsjournal.com.* (accessed October 1, 2013).
[14] Etan Azani, "Hezbollah's Global reach." *Hearing of the House Committee on International Relations— Subcommittee on International Terrorism and Nonproliferation.* Washington, D.C., September 2006.

effective, both internally and externally. In 2011, twelve Hezbollah agents were elected to the Lebanese parliament (out of 128), and Great Britain now recognizes the political arm of Hezbollah as a non-terror organization. A testament to the effectiveness of Hezbollah's information campaign is that while the world debates Hezbollah's organization and intent, Hezbollah's leadership maintains a clear purpose. "The organization's senior members have clarified more than once that Hezbollah and all of its branches are a single organic unit whose policy and activity are decided by its leadership."[15]

Among extremist-terrorist organizations, Hezbollah has blazed a new path in the synergistic use of terror, military capabilities, social action, criminal activity, information manipulation and political endeavors. Furthermore, while Lebanon is not an ungoverned space or failed state, Hezbollah, through forging all of these capabilities to common purpose, has inserted itself as *the* dominating influence in large swaths of Lebanon, allowing it virtually unfettered freedom of action. Within this multifaceted dynamic may reside the greatest capability, and threat, presented by Hezbollah. Through its political position, Hezbollah possesses legitimacy and broad based domestic and international support due to its deception of true design.

Cartels & Gangs

Mexican drug cartels and Latin gangs present a security threat throughout the western hemisphere. To some the concern is a law enforcement issue; to others it presents a grave threat to the security and stability of states. These groups continue to prosper at unprecedented levels and now dominate large geographic areas despite efforts

---

[15] *Ibid.*

to counter them. Of primary concern is that these groups have increased their range of operations, defying national and international efforts to subdue them. "Established crime groups have developed in Asia, Latin America, Africa, Europe, and the United States; no region of the world, nor any political system, has prevented their emergence, or succeeded in suppressing them."[16]

Once considered simply as drug trafficking organizations, cartels and gangs also prosper in the illicit transit of a variety of goods, most specifically human trafficking. "Unable to legally enter the developed countries of Western Europe and the United States, human smuggling rings run by international organized crime groups have arisen to meet the increased demand."[17] For the United States, this trafficking is primarily in the form of Central American and Mexican illegal immigrants, but it also contains elements of the sex trade while raising the specter of terrorist infiltration.[18]

In Mexico and across large swaths of Latin America, gangs and cartels have manipulated the gap opened up by weak governance to take control of large areas, which serve to facilitate their operations. "The new transnational crime groups, often operating regionally, exploit porous borders and dysfunctional state institutions where territory is outside the control of the central state."[19] This often develops into a self-supporting relationship. As TOCs gain more operational freedom due to their influence on local and

---

[16] Shelley, *The Unholy Trinity.*
[17] *Ibid.*
[18] Gertz, Bill. *Hizbullah building terror infrastructure in U.S., infiltrating from Mexico.* June 10, 2010. http://worldtribune.com/worldtribune/WTARC/2010/ss_terror0516_06_11.asp (accessed November 25, 2013).
   Enos, Olivia. *Crime-Ridden Mexican Border Fosters Human Trafficking.* August 11, 2011. http://blog.heritage.org/2011/08/11/crime-ridden-mexican-border-fosters-human-trafficking/ (accessed November 25, 2013).
   Human trafficking in Mexico targets women and children. January 2013, 2010. http://www.cnn.com/2010/WORLD/americas/01/13/mexico.human.traffic.drug/index.html (accessed November 25, 2013).
[19] Shelley, *The Unholy Trinity.*

regional governance, they are able to expand their enterprises and profits. This, in turn, provides more power and money to establish greater control and influence over expanding areas of influence. "Flush with increasing resources, political protection and access to law enforcement entities, the criminal organizations are ascendant."[20]

In Guatemala, Honduras, and El Salvador (the "Northern Triangle"), cartels and gangs have taken this span of influence, power and control to a new level, such that they pose a serious existential threat to the national governments. "…the Northern Triangle is emerging as a region where the state is often no longer the main power center or has become so entwined with a complex and inter-related web of illicit activities and actors that the state itself at times becomes a part of the criminal enterprise."[21] While the countries that comprise the Northern Triangle have long struggled to maintain adequate governing capacity, the introduction of TOCs to their territories could be the harbinger of a plummet into true failed-state status. "The result [from TOC influence] has been that the three governments have moved beyond being weak, somewhat corrupt and unresponsive to almost non-functional in much of their national territories."[22] This collapse, or near collapse, provides TOCs and others increased freedom, allowing them to more deeply entrench themselves in the region.

Recently, it has become clear that cartels and gangs are developing into multi-faceted organizations. This includes a variety of elements, which go beyond simple area control, and includes the recognition of the value of social support, which facilitates secure operating bases as well as a degree of legitimacy—at least among the local population.

---

[20] Farah, *Central America's Northern Triangle,* 89.
[21] *Ibid.,* 90.
[22] *Ibid.,* 89.

Vast swaths of national territory, the legal economy and government infrastructure now fall under the control of non-state actors whose budgets often rival or surpass those of the governments. …major drug trafficking leaders have acquired massive land holdings and provide employment, occasional medical care, educational services and other economic benefits to those on their land or adjacent villages. This, in turn, builds a solid social network that protects the traffickers from surprise raids or other state activities.[23]

In addition to the evolving dynamic nature of these illicit groups, they are beginning to recognize the value in working with other like-minded organizations. Mexican cartels are moving into the Northern Triangle, largely to increase their operational flexibility and span of control. This expansion has led MS-13 and *Calle* 18 to discuss building relationships with the encroaching cartels, with the potential of "partnership."[24] The implications of these actions show an evolution in organizational structure within the gangs as well as a desire for greater reach and effect. "The gangs' transformation from loose associations of small-time criminals devoid of strategic long-term planning into more coherent syndicates has alarmed authorities in Guatemala, El Salvador, and Honduras — all three of which are seeing the encroachment of Mexican cartels on their territories."[25] The lack of government capability and authority in the Northern Triangle, in the face of well organized, ruthless and capable illicit groups—who have found common cause—provides an existential threat to the legitimate governments of Honduras, Nicaragua, and El Salvador and a significant national security concern to the United States.

Although Hezbollah and the TOCs of Central America have differing agendas, they have much in common. Most notably, they operate within nation states, yet enjoy

---

[23] *Ibid.*, 93.

[24] Jamie Dettmer, "MS-13 and Calle 18 Developing Strong Relationships with Drug Cartels." *Dialogo*, December 19, 2011.

[25] *Ibid.*

freedom of action due to the inability of the local governments to challenge their power. Additionally, both Hezbollah and TOCs have taken aggressive steps to establish and maintain control over the populations of these "ungoverned" spaces, realizing the critical role that they play in their existence. Further, particularly within the Northern Triangle there are two things that are of interest to both of these groups, drugs (money, and with it means and power) and access to the United States.

CHAPTER 3: THE NEXUS

Many in the United States recognize that TOCs, with their brutal practices and illicit trafficking, are a security concern. Few, however, consider Hezbollah as a threat to the United States due to its relative anonymity. Further, there is little consideration or recognition of the prospect of a nexus between Hezbollah and TOCs. Regardless of the disparate motivations of these groups, such an unholy relationship, and the capability that it represents, presents a great concern for U.S. security. While many discount the likelihood of such a relationship, there are numerous indications and examples that the link between Hezbollah and TOCs already exists. Illicit activity for fund raising, either purely for profit or to fund other endeavors, is a common interest where Hezbollah's and TOC's operations have already intersected. In both the South American Tri-Border Area[1] (TBA) and Central America's Northern Triangle, there is strong evidence of this linkage. "Hezbollah conspires with drug-trafficking networks in Mexico and Central and South America as a means of raising and laundering funds, sharing tactics and "reaching out and touching" U.S. territory."[2]

There are many reasons for this nexus, with one of the defining elements in this dynamic being the occupation of "ungoverned spaces." In these spaces, terror and TOC groups draw support from the local populations while also using them to conduct illicit fund-raising activities. Although the social support and dynamics are different between

---

[1] The TBA is the border region between Brazil, Argentina and Paraguay.

[2] Roger Noriega, *Hezbollah's strategic shift: A global terrorist threat.* March 20, 2013. http://www.aei.org/speech/foreign-and-defense-policy/regional/middle-east-and-north-africa/hezbollahs-strategic-shift-a-global-terrorist-threat/ (accessed February 11, 2014).

Hezbollah and TOCs, the operational freedom and local support that exist in their ungoverned space operating bases are vital to the success of both Hezbollah and TOCs.

Ungoverned Spaces

As any organization seeks freedom to operate, terror groups and TOCs also seek operational freedom: "These franchises operate in, and control, specific geographic territories which allow them to function in a relatively safe environment."[3] Since both terror groups and TOCs look for similar environments in which to operate, it is natural that their paths converge.

> Hezbollah has taken advantage of the lawless region of the Tri-Border Area. The lack of rule of law makes the TBA a haven for criminal syndicates and nefarious factions from every continent come and function without restraint. Hezbollah too, exploits the lack of vigilant or concerned law enforcement which permits free trade and fairly free movement across the borders of Paraguay, Brazil, and Argentina"[4]

This trend of illicit partnership is growing, fueled by destabilized and ungoverned spaces where both terror groups and TOCs prosper. "…militias in Lebanon and criminal armies in Mexico are part of a global pattern and not anomalies."[5] This pattern is self-perpetuating, as TOCs and terror groups often provide the fuel for destabilization, in order to create operational spaces. These actions come with grave implications for international security. "The milieu into which transnational crime, terrorism, and corruption merge is extremely threatening to the international order."[6]

---

[3] Douglass Farah, *Transnational Organized Crime, Terrorism, and Criminalized States in Latin America: An Emerging Tier-One National Security Priority*. (Carlisle Barracks, PA: U.S. Army War College Strategic Studies Institute, 2012): 2.

[4] Cyrus Miryekta, "Hezbollah in the Tri-Border Area of South America." *smallwarsjournal.com*. (accessed October 1, 2013).

[5] Richard Shultz & Roy Godson, *Adapting America's Security Paradigm and Security Agenda*. (Washington, D.C.: National Strategy Information Center, 2010).

[6] Louise Shelley, "The Unholy Trinity: Transnational Crime, Corruption, and Terrorism." *Brown Journal of World Affairs* XI, no. 2 (Winter/Spring 2005): 101-111.

Another Ungoverned Space: International Law

Non-state illicit groups enjoy a relative "no man's land" regarding international law. "Mezzanine[7] rulers generally lie beyond the scope of international law, arguing that they are subject only to the laws of their host state, however powerless its government is to enforce them."[8] This "operating area" for terror and TOC groups typically lies within ungoverned spaces (although in some cases, such as Lebanon, Hezbollah's influence in effect creates a "state within a state," producing a similar result) and is a result of the international standard, where nation states are responsible for activities that take place within their borders. As has been seen repeatedly in the post Cold War era, the standards of international law have struggled to adjust to the dynamic caused by the rise of non-state actors. "International law, which remains based on the Westphalian model of nation-states, has not kept pace with this challenge."[9]

Recognition of the need for adapting international law, with specific regard to national sovereignty of the weak or failed state, has been slow. This is due to a lack of recognition of the threat presented by terror and TOC groups. "The international community was not much troubled by the inability of some states to control all of their own territory when the consequences were only local, but ungoverned space is now being exploited by mezzanine actors to launch transnational terrorist attacks, interfere with international transportation, or destabilize governments, with devastating results for

---

[7] Authors Michael Crawford and Jami Miscik in their Foreign Affairs article, "The Rise of Mezzanine Rulers" describe non-state groups, specifically mentioning Hezbollah as the preeminent example, as those groups who attain power by interjecting themselves between a state's population and the government. They use the term "Mezzanine" to describe this concept.
[8] Jami Miscik & Michael Crawford, "The Rise of the Mezzanine Rulers: The New Frontier for International Law." Edited by Jr James F. Hoge. *Foreign Affairs* 89, no. 6 (November/December 2010): 123-132.
[9] *Ibid.*

international peace and stability."[10] The events of 9/11 have brought global recognition to this new threat, but as ungoverned spaces continue to develop, and illicit groups continue to occupy them, the international community has demonstrated little consensus or ability to address the concern.

The Westphalia inspired system of international law, while hampering effective action against terror and TOC groups, may simultaneously be emboldening them. A"…[F]actor that has favored mezzanine rulers is the increasing scrutiny governments have to endure from foreign media and the international community, which tends to make them more risk averse. Mezzanine rulers, on the other hand, are subject to limited accountability, domestically and internationally, and therefore are inclined to take greater risks."[11] By taking the governments of weak states to task through interstate pressure and other means, the international community is unwittingly weakening, and restraining the actions of, the body most in need of support. Conversely, the message sent to the illicit group is one where the formal state government is accountable, not the illicit group itself. The final element to this dysfunctional approach has to do with the situation when the host state has no ability to influence the actions of the resident illicit groups. This dynamic is evident in Lebanon, where Hezbollah enjoys freedom of action outside of Lebanese government control, and the Northern Triangle where cartels and gangs operate virtually unrestrained.

The fractured and piecemeal approach taken by the international community towards illicit non-state groups provides another seam. Even the close relationship between the United States and the United Kingdom does not allow for a like perspective

---

[10] *Ibid.,*129.
[11] *Ibid.,*128.

of the threat. While the U.S. lists Hezbollah as a terror group, the U.K. only lists

Hezbollah's military wing as a terror group, leaving its other elements unfettered to

conduct operations.[12]

> Since the early 1990s, Hezbollah has been very concerned with public and
> international opinion. It has developed a well-oiled propaganda machine which
> has successfully blurred its image to the outside world. Because Hezbollah
> conducts propaganda and political warfare so well, using a two-pronged approach
> of coercion and persuasion, it has solidified much support in Lebanon, and is now
> vying for global opinion. These misconceptions, however, have severe
> implications. The world is divided on what the nature of Hezbollah is, which
> prevents efforts to counter it.[13]

This lack of international consensus on threat definition leads to uncoordinated actions,

resulting in limited effect. "The disparity between countries' domestic counterterrorism

legislation helps Hezbollah because it inhibits a consistent, unified Western response to

its activities."[14]

Establishing & Debating the Nexus

With the physical intersection of terror group and TOC operations, the nexus

between them was virtually inevitable. Both groups seek out and thrive in chaotic

environments. Both Hezbollah and TOCs have vast resources that allow them in some

cases to challenge regional and state authority, where they establish operating zones that

are largely free of influence by legitimate authorities.

Terror groups and TOCs, demonstrating pragmatic opportunism, have shown

themselves to be willing and able to build relationships with each other, based off mutual

benefit. "Rather than operating in isolation, these groups have complex but significant

action with each other, based primarily on the ability of each actor or set of actors to

---

[12] *Ibid.,* 124-125.
[13] Miryekta, *Hezbollah in the Tri-Border Area of South America.*
[14] Miscik & Crawford, *The Rise of the Mezzanine Rulers*, 125.

provide a critical service while profiting mutually from transactions."[15] Drug cartels and gangs, with their well-developed networks and infrastructures in Mexico and Latin America, provide access to those that would commit acts of terror against the U.S. Homeland.

Some argue that criminal organizations are unlikely to collaborate with terror groups due to the threat terror groups pose to the operating environment of the TOCs. The associated logic is generally that the objectives of terror groups are ultimately detrimental to criminal organizations; the actions of terror groups, and resulting state responses could result in damage to the criminal organizations. This may have been the case in the past, where international crime was dominated by mafia style groups that operated by corrupting officials *within* a functioning state. That model has given way, in large part, to a new model for international crime. "The newer crime groups in ungovernable regions are now forging alliances with terrorist organizations; because the crime groups and terrorist organizations do not possess long-term financial strategies or long-term political horizons, neither the criminals nor the terrorists need fear ineffective and corrupt law enforcement regimes in conflict regions."[16] Further, "The newer crime groups most often linked to terrorism have no interest in a secure state. In fact, they promote grievances, because it is through the prolongation of conflict that they enhance their profits. There is no disincentive for them to cooperate with terrorists because they want neither stability nor a state that can control them."[17] This perspective, coupled with the environments that they inhabit, create, and haunt, provides an ideal opportunity for

---

[15] Farah, *Transnational Organized Crime*, 10.
[16] Shelley, *The Unholy Trinity*.
[17] David M. Malone & Mats Berdal, *Greed & Grievance: Economic Agendas in Civil Wars,* Boulder, CO: Lynne Rienner Publishers, 2000.

association with terror groups. "The terrorists, who for political reasons seek to destroy the existing system, thus share a common objective with criminals. Both thrive on the violence and the disorder of the state."[18]

Although Hezbollah has been operating in the TBA since the 1980s, its recent activity in the Northern Triangle is of acute concern. This comes largely from the development of relationships with regional TOC groups who occupy a dominant position in the three-state region. "Para-state actors such as Hezbollah, the premier hybrid terrorist-TOC organization in the world, have been active in carrying out criminal activities in Central America, as documented by ongoing field research and multiple cases now in U.S. courts."[19] With Hezbollah in close operational proximity to TOCs, who exist largely to smuggle drugs, people, and other illicit items into the United States, there is a real concern that this nexus presents a clear and present danger to the United States. Former Drug Enforcement Agency (DEA) Executive Michael Braun, in 2012 testimony to the U.S. Congress, comprehensively illustrates this threat.

> These bad guys (cartels) are now routinely coming in very close contact with the likes of Hezbollah, Hamas, Al Qaeda, who are vying for the same money, the same turf and same dollars. It's really a nightmare scenario. And my point being is if anyone thinks for a moment that Hezbollah and Qods Force, the masters at leveraging and exploiting existing illicit infrastructures globally, are not going to focus on our southwest border and use that as perhaps a spring board in attacking our country then they just don't understand how the real underworld works.[20]

Despite the warnings offered by experts such as former agent Braun, many question whether gangs or cartels would be motivated to affiliate and work with terror groups due to an issue of organizational interest. "…[A]bsent a significant precipitating

---

[18] Shelly, *The Unholy Trinity.*

[19] Farah, *Central America's Northern Triangle*, 92.

[20] U.S. Congress, Committee on Homeland Security Hearing, *Iran, Hezbollah, and the Threat to the Homeland.* 112th Congress, March 21, 2012.

development in the Middle East, the likelihood of a terrorist attack on the United States by Hezbollah in the near future remains low.[21] Despite this dismissal and in concert with agent Braun's warning, the October 2011 attack on the Saudi Arabian Ambassador to the United States is instructive.

In October 2011 the Iranian Qods Force attempted to hire a Zeta Cartel member to assassinate the Saudi Ambassador to the United States for $1.5 million. While the assassination attempt was troubling in itself, there are indications that the relationship between Qods, Hezbollah, and Mexican Cartels is deeper than previously thought.

> In 2010, U.S. authorities accused Lebanese native Ayman Joumaa of selling Colombian cocaine to the Mexican Zetas drug cartel and laundering money for the drug-trafficking organization and channeling the profits to Hezbollah. The Zetas, one of Mexico's most ruthless cartels, also was in the news in October 2011, when U.S. officials said Iranian operatives tried to recruit cartel members to assassinate a Saudi diplomat in Washington.[22]

The investigation and subsequent indictment into Joumaa's actions further exposed the marriage of Iranian and Hezbollah interests and Mexican Cartels. "The indictment further substantiates the established relationship between Hezbollah, a proxy for Iran, and Mexican drug cartels, which control secured smuggling routes into the United States. This nexus potentially provides Iranian operatives with undetected access into the United States."[23]

With increasing familiarity and knowledge of Latin America, Hezbollah and its Iranian allies have proven able and willing to operate with and *manipulate* TOCs in order

---

[21] Arthur Brice, "Iran, Hezbollah mine Latin America for revenue, recruits, analysts say." *cnn.com.* June 3, 2013. http://www.cnn.com/2013/06/03/world/americas/iran-latin-america/index.html (accessed October 1, 2013).
[22] *Ibid.*
[23] Rep. Michael T. McCaul, *A Line in the Sand: Countering Crime, Violence and Terror at the Southwest Border.*)Washington, D.C.: U.S. House of Representatives, House Committee on Homeland Security, 2012), 9.

to support their agenda. "Iran and Hezbollah have been involved in the underworld of Latin America long enough to become intimately familiar with all of its inhabitants and capitalize on their capabilities."[24] Again, the 2011 assassination attempt upon the Saudi Ambassador to the U.S. supports this point. The Qods Force agents selected the cartel members because they knew that "drug traffickers are willing to undertake such activity in exchange for money."[25] Further, "…if this terror attack had been successful, the Qods Force intended to use Los Zetas for other attacks in the future."[26] Finally, a DEA representative testified in November 2011 that the alleged plot "illustrates the extent to which terrorist organizations will align themselves with other criminals to achieve their goals."[27] The example of the attempted assassination of the Saudi Ambassador provides an example of using a violent criminal agent to carry out a terror agenda item. It is easy to imagine Hezbollah manipulating gang or cartel members to conduct an act of terror in the future. While the above example illustrates the use of a proxy to commit acts of terror, it also clearly shows that Hezbollah and Iran are making use of TOCs to transport personnel (and presumably the tools of their trade) into the United States.

A Greater Concern

Hezbollah/Iranian presence in Latin America constitutes a clear threat to the security of the U.S. homeland…. In addition to operational terrorist activity, Hezbollah also is immersed in criminal activity throughout the region – from trafficking in weapons, drugs, and persons…. If our government and responsible partners in Latin America fail to act, I believe

---

[24] *Ibid.,*13.

[25] *U.S. v. Manssor Arbabsiar and Gholam Shakuri.* 1:11-cr-00897-JFK (U.S. District Court for the Southern District of New York). & Rep. McCaul, *A Line in the Sand.*
Note: The plot failed due to U.S. intervention—largely due to the work of undercover agents infiltrating the Zetas—not due to lack of Zeta interest.

[26] *U.S. v. Manssor Arbabsiar and Gholam Shakuri.*

[27] Sullivan Biettel, *Latin America: Terrorism Issues.* (Washington D.C.: Congressional Research Service, 2013).

there will be an attack on U.S. personnel, installations or interests in the Americas...[28]

With the intersection of Hezbollah's and TOCs interests and operations in the Northern Triangle, there is a particularly compelling concern: Should Hezbollah desire to move agents or capabilities into the United States, the trafficking capabilities of Mexican Cartels or Salvadorian Gangs could be of great assistance. "These networks are functioning, as Hezbollah smuggles its terrorists into the United States taking the Mexican drug routes."[29] Compounding this concern is the potential movement of Weapons of Mass Destruction (WMD) into the U.S. by Hezbollah. "Of equal concern is the possibility to smuggle materials, including uranium, which can be safely assembled on U.S. soil into a weapon of mass destruction."[30]

Considering the existential relationship between Hezbollah and Iran, and the long running animosity between the United States and Iran, Iran's nuclear ambitions bring a specter of great concern to the discussion. "How this plays into the Iranian nuclear threat leaves troubling possibilities for the U.S. and our ally Israel. We know that Hezbollah has a significant presence in the United States that could be utilized in terror attacks intended to deter our efforts to curtail Iran's nuclear program."[31] Roger Noriega, former Assistant Secretary of State for Western Hemisphere Affairs offers a nuanced, similar warning, which suggests Hezbollah's desire for anonymity in attacking the United States. "If our government and responsible partners in Latin America fail to act, I believe there will be an attack on U.S. personnel, installations or interests in the Americas as soon as

---

[28] Noriega, *Hezbollah's strategic shift.*
[29] Sara Carter, "Exclusive: Hezbollah uses Mexican drug routes into U.S." *Washington Times*, March 27, 2009.
[30] Rep. McCaul, *A Line in the Sand*, 3.
[31] U.S. Congress, *Iran, Hezbollah, and the Threat to the Homeland.* As quoted by, Rep. McCaul, *A Line in the Sand*, 15.

Hezbollah operatives believe that they are capable of such an operation without implicating their Iranian sponsors in the crime."[32]

The capability and function of Hezbollah, with weapons developed by Iran, facilitated by the illicit transit networks of TOCs, combine to present a nightmare scenario for the United States.

---

[32] Ryan Mauro, *Growing Hezbollah Presence in Southwest U.S.* October 13, 2013. http://m.clarionproject.org/analysis/hezbollah-tattoos-increasing-found-us-prison-inmates (accessed February 11, 2014).

CHAPTER 4: CURRENT U.S. GOVERNMENT ACTIVITIES

Three U.S. national strategies deal (broadly) with the issue of the nexus between Hezbollah and TOCs. These are the National Security Strategy (NSS), published in 2010, the National Strategy for Counterterrorism, published in 2011, and the Strategy to Combat Transnational Organized Crime, also published in 2011. While all of these strategies reference the issue of a terror-criminal nexus in rough form, none of them address the concern directly. Significantly, there is minimal discussion of Hezbollah, while TOC discussion focuses upon international organized crime as an item generally isolated from terrorism.

With the 2011 release of The Strategy to Combat Transnational Organized Crime, the President and National Security Council (NSC) identified the high level of concern that is provoked by TOC groups. The strategy recognizes that the solution to this threat is dynamic and will require both interagency and international efforts. "This Strategy is organized around a single unifying principle: to build, balance, and integrate the tools of American power to combat transnational organized crime and related threats to national security—and to urge our foreign partners to do the same."[1] Recognition of this threat, and the dynamic challenge it presents is overdue.

To be certain, the Federal government operates on many fronts against both terrorism and transnational crime. The approach, however, appears to be largely one of independent agencies acting as they see fit, rather than in a coordinated and comprehensive effort. Although there have been recent success in countering terrorism,

---

[1] National Security Council, *Strategy to Combat Transnational Organized Crime: Addressing Converging Threats to National Security,* (Washington, D.C., 2011).

events in Pakistan, Iraq, Mali, Libya, Somalia, and numerous other nations indicate that terror groups, including Al Qaeda, have not been critically harmed and will continue their operations. Additionally, there is little or no evidence of U.S. targeting of Hezbollah in any form.[2] Similarly, transnational organized crime groups, although under some pressure due to impacts surrounding the U.S. border with Mexico, are operating with extraordinary freedom in Central and South America.

The following is a brief discussion of some of the U.S. Government's efforts to counter terror and TOC groups, and where these efforts fall short.[3]

Department of State

The DOS has numerous long-term counterterrorism programs. Among the more notable are the Anti-Terrorism Assistance Program (ATA), the Countering Violent Extremism (CVE), and the Global Counterterrorism Forum (GCTF).[4]

The ATA, created in 1983, has provided training and equipment to law enforcement agencies of partner nations. Its focus has been on improving overall law enforcement capacity as well as promoting regional coordination and cooperation, among other things. Central to its intent, the ATA strongly emphasizes the rule of law and human rights.[5]

---

[2] It is fully appreciated that a vast amount of counterterror and counter TOC efforts and information are not available as open source. In fact, the expectation is that virtually all intelligence and military information related to these issues is not available via open source and thus will not be addressed in detail in this paper.

[3] This is not a comprehensive nor exhaustive list, but is simply intended to show the reader some of the capabilities and initiatives that these agencies are exercising. Additionally, as noted previously, DOD and Intelligence Agency efforts will not be discussed in detail largely due to their classified nature. Also, it is fairly common knowledge that these agencies have a heavy focus upon Direct Action (DA), through the use of manned and unmanned aircraft as well as special operations and similar forces. Law enforcement efforts are also commonly understood in the main and will not be covered in detail.

[4] Please see www.state.gov for full details of these and other related programs.

[5] Department of State. *www.state.gov/j/ct/programs/index.htm#ctf.* (accessed January 3, 2014).

The CVE is a pillar of the current administration's approach to counterterrorism. It provides grants to foreign nations to support three main lines of effort:

1) To provide positive alternatives to those most at-risk of radicalization and recruitment into violent extremism;
2) Counter violent extremist narratives and messaging; and
3) Increase international partner capacity (civil society and government) to address the drivers of radicalization.[6]

The CVE strays somewhat from "traditional diplomacy" as it focuses upon communities and law enforcement in finding ways to prevent radicalization of "at risk" populations. This includes identification and elimination of problems within a community that could enhance vulnerability to radicalization and recruitment through a variety of means, including the use of mentors and community leaders.

The GCTF (launched in 2011) is designed to support nations in developing rule of law (and related) capabilities and capacity building with specific focus upon countering violent extremism. This forum has seen successes in the development of several memorandums (Rabat, Rome, and Algiers) where partner nations have agreed to efforts supporting rule of law, effective counterterrorism practice, reintegration of violent extremists, and other related topics.[7]

DOS has also, as part of the 2011 Strategy to Combat Transnational Crime, launched several initiatives to support rule of law efforts of local governments in combatting TOCs. Notable among these is the, "Central America Regional Security Initiative to coordinate investigations, support prosecutions, and build our collective capacity to identify, disrupt, and dismantle transnational organized crime groups."[8] As

---

[6] Department of State.
[7] *Ibid.*
[8] William J. Burns, *Statement by Under Secretary for Political Affairs William J. Burns*, 25 July 2011. *www.state.gov/p/us/rm/2011/169045.htm#.* July 25, 2011. (accessed January 3, 2014).

part of the President's new counter-TOC strategy, this initiative establishes a new sanctions program against specified TOC groups and a cash rewards program[9] that provides incentive to those willing to come forward with information that leads to the arrest or conviction of TOC members.

Treasury Department

As would be expected, the Treasury Department's contribution to counterterrorism and countering TOC groups centers upon financial targeting. Under the heading of "Terrorism and Illicit Finance," the Treasury Department describes that it, "…performs a critical and far-reaching role in enhancing national security by implementing economic sanctions against foreign threats to the U.S., identifying and targeting the financial support networks of national security threats, and improving the safeguards of our financial systems."[10] The Treasury Department has strongly embraced its role in national security, particularly with the establishment of the Counterterrorism Section (CTS), which, "is responsible for the design, implementation, and support of law enforcement efforts, legislative initiatives, policies and strategies relating to combatting international and domestic terrorism."[11]

Perhaps the most well known of the Treasury Department's efforts are the financial sanctions against terror and criminal agents. Similar to sanctions are the Asset Forfeiture[12] program targeting the assets of both terror and TOC members. The design of both the sanctions and forfeiture programs recognizes that financial assets are critical to the operations and support of these illicit groups and that undermining them can have a

---

[9] Department of State.

[10] Treasury Department. *www.treasury.gov/resource-center/terrorist-illicit-finance/pages/default.aspx.* (accessed January 3, 2014).

[11] *Ibid.*

[12] *Ibid.*

significant impact upon their capabilities. A third program targeting illicit finances is Treasury's Money Laundering program where Treasury targets the organizations and networks that launder money for illicit groups.[13]

Another program of note is the Terrorist Finance Tracking Program (TFTP). Treasury initiated this program, "to identify, track, and pursue terrorists and their networks."[14] Along a similar line in Treasury's arsenal of counterterror and counter-TOC activities are the Hawala and Alternative Remittance Systems.[15] The Hawala program recognizes the unique Islamic Hawala financial system, which terror groups use to hide, launder, and distribute money. Similarly, by investigating remittances, Treasury targets illicit money sent out of the U.S. by TOC agents.

Homeland Security & Justice

In most situations, the Departments of Homeland Security and Justice (DHS and DOJ, respectively) play the "home game" against both the terror threat and TOCs. The efforts conducted by both DHS and DOJ focus upon domestic law enforcement, which routinely incorporates State and Local law enforcement agencies.[16] DHS and DOJ are the primary agencies waging the lesser noticed "daily fight" against both terror and TOC agents through conduct of their law enforcement duties and control of U.S. borders and littorals (Border Police, Immigration and Customs Enforcement, and the U.S. Coast Guard). A prime example of their effective operations was the interception of the

---

[13] *Ibid.*

[14] *Ibid.* There is a similar effort at the DOS called Counterterrorism Finance (CTF), which also tracks financial leads while seeking to deny access to financial systems and resources.

[15] *Ibid.*

[16] The author's brother is an FBI agent who works as part of a combined counter-gang task force in Southern California. Virtually all of his work is done in the form of a Federal, State and Local law enforcement task force.

Qods/Los Zetas plot against the Saudi Ambassador where the Drug Enforcement Agency (DEA—a component of DOJ) played a central role.

Gaps in Government Efforts

Missing from current counterterrorism and counter-TOC efforts is a common understanding of the problem and a unified approach. Few dispute the threat presented by these groups separately. It is clear, however, that these illicit groups are already working together. Addressing these concerns together will require a binding directive, which establishes the bridge between terror and TOC groups while stipulating that separate Federal agencies coordinate their programs and initiatives at all levels.

A most basic requirement for a successful approach is recognition of the objective while focusing resources against those issues, which create the problem or threat, "…strategy focuses on root causes and purposes."[17] While this seems intuitive, actual recognition of the threat and its attendant dynamics is often illusive. For example, U.S. efforts against terror groups tend to focus upon elimination of terror cells and individuals, not upon the factors that create and enable terrorists. Similarly, efforts against cartels and gangs focus upon interception of drugs and incarceration of group members, and not upon the factors that allow gangs and cartels to recruit and prosper. While DA and actions designed to get terror and gang members "off the street" are valid, the U.S., and the international community must address the causal and enabling factors supporting and sustaining terror groups and TOCs.

---

[17] Harry R. Yarger, *Strategic Theory for the 21st Century: The Little Book on Big Strategy.* (Carlisle, PA: Strategic Studies Institute, U.S. Army, 2006).

Existing U.S. strategies against terrorism and transnational organized crime illustrate strong, and increasing, recognition of these threats. Terrorism has been a front line concern for decades (admittedly, with varying levels of attention and effort applied against it). TOC groups are a more recently recognized concern, but the 2011 TOC strategy shows an important growth in understanding of the threat presented by these groups. These strategies fall short, however, in four ways.

First, it could be argued that of these three strategies, only the National Security Strategy would qualify as a true strategy. While both the National Counterterrorism Strategy and Counter-TOC strategies nest underneath the NSS, they provide more of a focused approach to dealing with their respective concerns. Second, references to Hezbollah are virtually in passing. As previously discussed, Hezbollah's advanced capability is striking, not to mention that it enjoys the backing of a regional power with an emergent nuclear program. Third, all U.S. security strategies fail to acknowledge that Hezbollah and TOC groups have begun to collaborate, and in many functional ways resemble each other—clouding the distinction between them. Hezbollah operates a variety of illicit (drug) fundraising networks and uses social programs to garner popular support. TOCs, meanwhile, use murder and intimidation (terror) to control governments and populations. They also make social outreach efforts designed to gain popular support, while also using them to discredit area governance. Although the motivations of terror groups and TOCs are different, the techniques they employ, environments in which they operate, and the relationships they are developing between each other indicate significant commonality. Finally, these strategies do not present a unified U.S. and international effort against Hezbollah and TOCs. Much discussion is dedicated to the "interagency approach," yet the preponderance of action is taken within independent agencies (let alone individual nations) with limited concern for implications across the spectrum of interested parties and the second and third order implications of their actions on the greater problem.

As troubling as this illicit synergy is, there is reason to see this as opportunity. Methods, which prove effective against one group, could actually damage another due to their inter-relationship. Similarly, methods validated against one group, and *properly applied*[18] against another, could have positive effect.

---

[18] It is important to note that tactics effective against one group can have positive effect against another. The issue is appropriate adjustment of these tactics to the target. Successful information and anti-corruption campaigns in Central America will need to be substantially revisited in order have similar effect in Lebanon.

CHAPTER 5: DEVELOPING A COMPREHENSIVE INTERAGENCY & INTERNATIONAL APPROACH

U.S. federal agencies must recognize that national security requires a comprehensive effort. National security goes beyond DOD, DHS, DOJ and the Intelligence community. The Department of State must fully embrace a primary role in providing national security. Furthermore, contributions from other federal agencies (such as the Departments of Energy or Education) may also support the DOS effort, providing valuable skills and insight in addressing root causes. These contributions are such that they can address the conditions, outside and inside U.S. borders, which allow illicit groups to recruit, operate and prosper.

The U.S. approach must have full realization that this is a complex, *wicked* problem. "Now we are faced with a new threat in Latin America that comes from the growing collaborations between Iran, Venezuela, Hezbollah and transnational criminal organizations. Similar to the Cuban Missile Crisis, the evidence to compel action exists; the only question is whether we possess the imagination to connect the dots before another disaster strikes."[1] U.S. assets must operate as part of an integrated strategic approach that produces complimentary effects rather than disparate ones. "Western policymakers should seek to address the problem systematically, at both a strategic political and a legal level, rather than continue to pursue disjointed reactive measures on a case-by-case basis. Policymakers will need to confront, rather than shirk, strategic complexities."[2] The example of Hezbollah illustrates this perspective perfectly. "By mixing religion, ideology, social welfare, politics and occasional violence, Hezbollah has

---

[1] Rep. McCaul, *A Line in the Sand*, 3.
[2] Miscik & Crawford, *The Rise of the Mezzanine Rulers*, 132.

gained legitimacy with local communities and developed sophisticated institutional

practices, which give it strength and resilience. The movement is at once a religious

organization, a political party, and a paramilitary force."[3] Since Hezbollah is at once

religious, political and paramilitary, any efforts directed against it will require an

integrated approach that targets weaknesses, while degrading or minimizing its strengths.

Additionally, Hezbollah's organizational resiliency will require U.S. agencies to develop

a plan that addresses the threat from multiple aspects simultaneously. Piecemeal,

uncoordinated efforts will have little likelihood of lasting success.

　　　　To avoid dealing with the same threat in perpetuity, the approach must address

root causes. In cases where non-state entities are the concern, the host nation/ungoverned

spaces should be the central focus, with the intention of building host nation capability to

combat the threat. Essentially the U.S. (and international partners) will be doing three

things at once; preventing attacks upon the homeland, addressing root causes and

associated factors, and building host/partner nation capability to first contribute, and then

carry the effort themselves.

A method for addressing a Hezbollah-TOC nexus is through "threat rings." These rings are not geographic, but conceptual. The

Photo Removed Due to Copyright Restrictions

---

[3] *Ibid.,* 124.

intent is to recognize the threat, develop specific actions at each level to address different aspects of the threat, and to ensure integration of efforts between levels. These "threat rings" start with the outermost, the "Engagement" ring, then move to the middle "Interdiction" ring, and finally the inner "Intercept" ring. These rings serve as lenses for government agencies to consider their role in the approach. These rings are separate yet fluid and linked, focusing on specific actions, while considering broader implications.

The focus of effort in the Engagement Ring is use of non-military capabilities, with specific focus on enabling and prompting the host nation to action. The middle "Interdiction Ring" focuses upon stopping the threat as it transits between havens or to the United States (or an Ally). In most cases, these interdiction activities will be intelligence driven, with actions taken by military, intelligence or law enforcement capabilities. Additionally, these actions are in large part intended to be the responsibility of host nation intelligence and security forces. The U.S. may enable these host nation efforts through a variety of Engagement Ring activities, including Security Force Assistance (SFA), Building Partner Capacity (BPC), as well as law enforcement exchanges. Further, while certain U.S. elements are conducting Interdiction Ring operations, DOS elements would be facilitating host nation support. The inner ring is the "Intercept" ring—the final line of defense within the United States or its immediate borders (sea or land) where military, law enforcement or intelligence capabilities will be used to prevent an imminent attack.

The example of SFA and BPC initiatives providing a baseline for military or law enforcement direct action illustrates the fluid and complementary nature of the separate levels, while also exhibiting that actions in different rings can and will be taking place at the same time and in the same space. Efforts taken without understanding their relationship to, and impact upon, other aspects of the approach are likely to negatively impact the overall effort. Such an example is the U.S.'s use of drone strikes against Al Qaeda targets. While few doubt the immediate effect of the strikes in killing terror agents, there is debate over the true impact of the strikes. Indeed, popular sentiment in Muslim nations against drone strikes suggests that drone strikes in Pakistan and Yemen are actually counterproductive to the overall end state of destroying Al Qaeda.

Engagement Ring

The Engagement ring is the most significant of the three rings, where U.S. influence and power focuses upon root causes and prevention. This ring has two basic elements. First, the efforts of the international community must be galvanized. This includes the requirement to address the existing system of international law as it pertains to ungoverned spaces (or ineffectively governed spaces), as well as non-state groups.[4] In essence, international law must prevent non-state actors, such as Hezbollah and TOCs, to enjoy protection from the law due to the law's State-centric model. International law must adjust to hold non-state groups responsible for their actions. The second element of this ring is composed of the multi-faceted actions that the U.S. and the international community will take towards a state or non-state actor in order to eliminate a threat.

---

[4] These efforts, from the U.S. perspective, must recognize long-term implications and be within the constraints set forward by the Constitution. For full discussion please see:
  Jon Kyl, Douglas J. Feith, & John Fonte. "The War of Law: How New International Law Undermines Democratic Sovereignty." Edited by Gideon Rose. *Foreign Affairs* (Lynda Hammes) 92, no. 4 (July/August 2013): 115-125.
  Alexander Hamilton, John Jay, & James Madison. *The Federalist Papers.* (Metairie, LA: Megalodon Entertainment LLC, 2010).
    Practitioners must be mindful of James Madison's comments in Federalist Number 46, (Madison) "…the ultimate authority, wherever the derivative may be found, resides in the people alone,…" In attempting to make international law that is more responsive to non-state related concerns, U.S. agents must consider the potential for future use of such tenets against U.S. interests.

These elements require a significant degree of host-nation support to be successful. The U.S. and international partners can engage Hezbollah and TOCs from international positions, but to have a lasting solution, the effort will require domestic support. Admittedly, in both the cases of Lebanon and the Northern Triangle, local governments have limited ability to affect either Hezbollah or the TOCs.

To begin the campaign against Hezbollah, the United States must find ways to work with its Allies towards a common end; finding areas of agreement will lead to combined action. While the U.S. and others may disagree on Hezbollah and its varied positions, viewing the problem through a lens of criminal behavior could be the key to progress. "So while there is no common understanding between the United States and the United Kingdom on whether or how to engage Hezbollah or even how to classify Hezbollah and its various component parts, there is no 'gray area' as to whether drug trafficking is illegal."[5] This common understanding could provide opportunity for expanded discussion between the United States and others to address the concerns that Hezbollah presents as it operates with and among TOCs.

Addressing the nexus between Hezbollah and TOCs will require Americans, Europeans, and other partner nations to recognize the need for evolved thought. "The destabilizing nexus of transnational crime and terrorism has proved so intractable because policy-makers continue to think about crime in terms of traditional paradigms."[6] Those that construct policy and strategy must first recognize the need for review of existing concepts for both content and structure. A strategy for counterterrorism and a separate strategy for international criminal organizations by themselves will not provide a bridge

[5] Mathew Levitt, *Hezbollah: Narco-Islamism.* (Washington, D.C.: The Washington Institute for Near East Policy, 2009).
[6] Shelley, *The Unholy Trinity.*

for an interagency, much less an international plan to address the problem. Similarly, compromise in trans-Atlantic perspectives will be necessary to ensure progress in addressing the terror-TOC nexus through international efforts. "American policy-makers in the post 9/11 world have focused almost exclusively on terrorism, whereas their European counterparts have focused much more on transnational crime."[7] Current global thinking and paradigms have been insufficient in addressing the rise of non-state illicit groups. To reduce them, new perspectives and approaches are necessary.

These discussions must include others in Asia and Africa, and specifically Central and South America. International law has traditionally been the purview of the West. With terror groups coming predominantly from the Mid-East and Africa, and TOCs frequently coming from Latin America, it is imperative that the U.S. and Europe recognize that other nations will play the determining role in defeating this emergent concern. Illustrating this is the belief that the best way to address militant Islamist groups is through the lens of Islam. "Militant Islamist Ideology can be fought only by using *Islamic* argumentation and exposing Militant Islamist views as narrow and doing a disservice to the legacy of Islam."[8]

Once international consensus is established, the international community will then need to take action. As has been discussed previously, Hezbollah's rise and status are in large part due to their highly effective media operations. Information, and manipulation of it, has been a key component to their success. Additionally, international scrutiny of

---

[7] *Ibid.*

[8] Youssef H. Aboul-Enein, *Militant Islamist Ideology: Understanding the Global Threat.* (Annapolis, Marlyand: Naval Institute Press, 2010), 12. Italics in original.
This concept is supported by a personal discussion with a Lebanese officer who attended the JFSC who suggested that the key to defeating Hezbollah was to "separate it from Shi'ism." Instead of addressing the Lebanese population with the desire of destroying the reputation of Hezbollah, the goal should be to expose the truth of Hezbollah as an apostate entity, one that uses the mantle of Islam to cover illicit activities.

Lebanon, and tacit acceptance of Hezbollah's non-military elements, have aided Hezbollah's rise. Thus, a strong first step would be to reverse the current dynamic. "Subjecting mezzanine rulers to greater international scrutiny is one way the West could do more. This would expose mezzanine rulers to outside influences and force them to justify their actions."[9] Reinforcing this would be an information campaign designed to discredit Hezbollah, with particular focus upon Islamic principles. "A carefully directed information campaign by the West could help cast a harsh light on the darker workings of mezzanine rulers. The deliberate erosion of the mezzanine actors' myths and cult of resistance will be vital to success."[10] This effort is essentially an information campaign designed to expose the truth of Hezbollah, first to the international community (to gather support), and then to Hezbollah's sanctuary, the Lebanese population.

Building the capability and legitimacy of the Lebanese government, specifically in its relationship with its population, is a defining aspect of the Engagement Ring's activities. "An important way to combat threats emanating from weak and fragile states is to strengthen legitimate government and the rule of law to alleviate pressures that lead to instability."[11] This would include SFA and BPC activities as well as domestic information, social and governance elements.

Actions against Hezbollah within Lebanon would also include a wider array of U.S. federal capabilities. The DOS would lead the effort, gaining access through the non-Hezbollah agents within the Lebanese government. These other capabilities would also

---

[9] Jami Miscik & Michael Crawford, "The Rise of the Mezzanine Rulers: The New Frontier for International Law." Edited by Jr James F. Hoge. *Foreign Affairs* 89, no. 6 (November/December 2010), 123-132.

[10] *Ibid.,* 132.

[11] Richard Shultz & Roy Godson, *Adapting America's Security Paradigm and Security Agenda.* (Washington, D.C.: National Strategy Information Center, 2010).

focus upon compromising Hezbollah's social standing by providing alternatives to their social outreach programs while using an information campaign to discredit Hezbollah while bolstering the legitimate aspects of the Lebanese government. These programs would be agricultural, educational, and importantly, religious.[12]

With many efforts directed against Hezbollah inside of Lebanon, there will also be external efforts designed to have a crippling effect. These include the financial targeting of Hezbollah's illicit financial network, one that stretches into the Western Hemisphere. "One such scheme involved the [Lebanese Canadian Bank] allowing Hezbollah-related entities to conduct transactions as large as $260,000 per day without disclosing any information about the transaction."[13] These actions must be continued and increased, with an expanded scope to include other banking centers such as the United Arab Emirates (UAE) and the Cayman Islands. Specifically when tracking Hezbollah's money trail in the Western Hemisphere there is the chance that there will be a financial intersection between Hezbollah and TOCs. Similarly, given the known use of the UAE as a haven for Iranian (not to mention other illicit groups, such as opium kingpins in Afghanistan) funds, there is good reason to believe that where Iranian assets are hidden, Hezbollah's assets may be present as well.

Another important Engagement Ring activity to defeat Hezbollah would be to drive a wedge between the religious beliefs of the population and Hezbollah's actions. If the actual agenda of Hezbollah and the non-Muslim actions it has taken were to be effectively exposed, it is likely that the result would be a serious compromise in their

---

[12] These efforts would be conducted by Lebanese elements with the support of USAID, Department of Agriculture, Department of Education and other federal agencies as able. Additionally, international partners, particularly Muslim nations and NGOs would be of great value in this effort.
[13] "Press Release, U.S. Attourney's Office for the Southern District of New York." December 15, 2011.

local base of support. The effort should center upon removing the veneer of Shi'ism from Hezbollah. There are clear signs that many Lebanese, including Shiites do not support Hezbollah's agenda, "In her widely translated article, "To Be a Shiite Now," Fayyad questioned the imposition of Hezbollah's ideology—and the consequences of Hezbollah's authority—over Shiites and Lebanon."[14] This effort hinges upon wresting the Islamic narrative from Hezbollah, and exposing it as in violation of Islam, as apostate. As has been learned repeatedly in recent conflicts in Iraq and Afghanistan, Islamist insurgents have proven adept at promoting their narrative of religion. While effective in garnering support, this narrative is in contrast to true Muslim doctrine. "Today Militant Islamists have been so proficient in the use of the media that the meaning and contributions of Islamic civilization have become lost not just in mainstream Western discourse but tragically in the Muslim world itself."[15]

The elements of an approach designed to reduce Hezbollah are similar to those used against TOCs in the Northern Triangle. As in targeting Hezbollah in Lebanon, many of the same societal dynamics exist in Guatemala, El Salvador and Honduras. "In these conflict regions, crime groups see business differently but also citizens see them as a major force in a large shadow economy. They provide goods and services as well as jobs not provided by the legitimate economy. Therefore, many citizens do not see crime groups in post-conflict regions as purely 'bad' but as groups that perform needed economic services for their community."[16] However, the application will vary considerably as the cultural and regional dynamics require a separate analysis. Most

---

[14] David Schenker, "Shiites Against Hezbollah." *The Weekly Standard*, 2006.
[15] Youssef H. Aboul-Enein, *Militant Islamist Ideology: Understanding the Global Threat.* (Annapolis, Marlyland: Naval Institute Press, 2010), 9.
[16] Shelley, *The Unholy Trinity.*

notably, while religion is central to defeating Hezbollah, religion in Central America, although a strong element of Latin culture, is unlikely to play the same role as it would in the Levant.

While TOCs lack the centralized capabilities of Hezbollah, the societal dynamics that exist in the Northern Triangle lend themselves to similar approaches. As previously discussed, the social aspect of TOC operations compromises the legitimacy of local governance while also providing a safe base of operations. Like efforts against Hezbollah, actions designed to dismantle TOC networks must be comprehensive. A primary theme must be to restore the legitimate ruling capabilities of the local government(s). Similar to a campaign against Hezbollah, the effort will include a robust information campaign designed to compromise the local popularity of the TOCs. Also like against Hezbollah, the approach must appreciate the diversity and resilience of the target. The U.S. has had success with such complex efforts in the past, most notably in Colombia. "The strategy required attacking every vulnerability of the trafficking organizations at every step of the process…"[17]

The successful U.S-Colombian counter-TOC model is seeing a revision and revival in current anti-cartel efforts in Mexico. Despite challenges with widespread corruption and tenacious cartel resistance, the Mexican government has seen positive progress. "Calderon's initiatives have begun to destabilize the cartels, and many cartel leaders are now on the run."[18] Perhaps as encouraging as the efforts of the Mexican government are the recent indications that segments of the Mexican population itself are no longer tolerating the cartels and their activities. In recent years, "The lawlessness

---

[17] Robert C. Bonner, "The New Cocaine Cowboys: How to Defeat Mexico's Drug Cartels." Edited by JR James F. Hoge. *Foreign Affairs* (David Kellogg) 89, no. 4 (July/August 2010): 35-47.
[18] *Ibid.*

spawned by Mexico's drug wars has contributed to the spread of self- defense groups,...."[19] This is encouraging due to the willingness of local populations to take action against illicit groups. Interestingly, this rise in vigilante justice appears to have come from a "tipping point" not unlike what was seen in the 2006, "Al Anbar Awakening." Like in Al Anbar, it appears that cartel actions against the local population, as opposed to the government, pushed the people into action. "Narcotraffickers as a rule usually keep things under control in their territories, but lately they've been getting involved in extortion and murders, and that's not right. The drug problem is for the state to resolve, but kidnapping and robbery touches us."[20] There is concern, however, that if taken too far, this vigilantism will further erode the tenuous rule of law in Mexico. Recognizing that a central component of defeating TOCs is the restoration of legitimate government authority, these concerns merit strong consideration. Despite this, the fact that local populations in Mexico are taking action against cartels is a positive indicator that could contribute to a wider effort to dismantle the TOCs operating in those areas. Simply, vigilante actions against TOCs indicate potential receptiveness of information and other efforts (such as economic development, anti-corruption campaigns and other government-social programs) aimed at destroying the cartels and the restoration of legitimate governance.

Interdiction Ring

The focus of the Interdiction Ring is to stop the flow of Hezbollah or TOC assets as they transit between waypoints or are within operational areas. In this ring,

---

[19] Ralph Espach & Patricio Asfura-Heim, "The Rise of Mexico's Self-Defense Forces: Vigilante Justice South of the Border." Edited by Gideon Rose. *Foreign Affairs* (Lynda Hammes) 92, no. 4 (July/August 2013): 143-150.
[20] A group leader in "Tierra Colorada" as quoted in: Espach & Asfura-Heim, *The Rise of Mexico's Self-Defense Forces.*

employment of direct action (DA) supports the overall effort—with close attention paid to the impacts it may have on Engagement efforts. Significantly, DA comes in many forms. Most dramatic is the use of Special Forces, other military, law enforcement, or intelligence personnel to *kill or capture* terror or criminal agents.

In conducting direct action missions, the difference between kill and capture is significant. This difference is in the risk to U.S. and Allied personnel, the intelligence value of a target, the messaging to other illicit group members and supporters, and the perceptions aroused by local, international and domestic audiences.

> Terrorist groups can meet their demise in a number of ways, and the killing of their leaders is certainly one of them. Abu Sayyaf, an Islamist separatist group in the Philippines, lost its political focus, split into factions, and became a petty criminal organization after the army killed its leaders in 2006 and 2007. In other cases, however, including those of the Shining Path in Peru and Action Directe in France, the humiliating arrest of a leader has been more effective. By capturing a terrorist leader, countries can avoid creating a martyr, win access to a storehouse of intelligence, and discredit a popular cause.[21]

In mission planning, considerations for intelligence collection, the potential for martyrdom, and local sentiment are crucial. Additionally, individual mission planning should evaluate how the mission relates to the overall approach. The relationship between U.S. direct action and its impact upon local governments has been significant in recent years. U.S. actions have often upset local populations and strained relations with the local governments. Pakistan is such an example, where both manned DA (Abbotabad and Osama Bin Laden), and numerous drone strikes have been unpopular with the population. This has resulted in Pakistani governmental and popular criticism and condemnation of the U.S. and its counterterrorism activities within Pakistan.

---

[21] Audrey Kurth Cronin, "Why Drones Fail: When Tactics Drive Strategy," Edited by Gideon Rose, *Foreign Affairs* (Lynda Hammes) 92, no. 4 (July/August 2013), 44-54.

The situation with Pakistan is instructive: How does the U.S. (or any other nation) target terror agents in a sovereign nation without drawing a backlash that could breed sympathy for the terrorist cause? Direct action interdiction missions have a premium requirement for effective application of international law. Like the challenges faced in conducting engagement, proper application of international law, and the corresponding legitimacy provided when operating within its mandates, will be critical in carrying out interdiction efforts. That international law struggles to deal with non-state groups complicates the issue greatly. Without effective elements of international law and international support, DA operations will remain highly contentious and divisive while being fodder for those savvy in the media and information domains.

This is particularly the case in targeting Hezbollah. Hezbollah has maintained a low-terror profile in recent years, making DA targeting by U.S. agents virtual "no-go terrain." Additionally, the political standing of its senior leadership gives it an air of legitimacy, making the targeting of figures such as Nasrallah an unacceptable prospect. Thus, as DA against Al Qaeda leadership has proven effective in degrading the organization, Hezbollah presents a significantly different challenge, which requires a well-justified approach in international law and associated consensus.

This targeting and international law concern is particularly acute with the use of drones. Drones, while particularly effective at hitting targets and keeping U.S. military and intelligence personnel safe, have become a highly contentious issue. Due to their remote nature and belief that they cause unacceptable "collateral damage," namely the deaths of relations and bystanders to the targets, the use of drones has come into question. Legal, ethical and most importantly, legitimacy, questions have made the use of drones a lightning rod of criticism of the United States from international and domestic audiences. The U.S. employment of drones in counter-terror or counter-criminal operations must be well coordinated with host nations and well justified both in the immediate targeting but also in a comprehensive view of the overall strategy. "Drone strikes must be legally justified, transparent and rare. Washington needs to better establish and follow a publicly explained legal and moral framework for the use of drones, making sure that they are part of a long-term political strategy that undermines the enemies of the United States."[22] While a tactical system, the drone has become a weapon with strategic effect. These strategic impacts, however, are often greater *against the user than the intended targets*. Thus, the U.S. must carefully consider each use of drone strikes and its overall impact on the approach. This broad-view calculus will often result in changing the mission timing, or changing the mission objective from kill to capture, in order to garner the desired immediate and second order effects, or to mitigate negative backlash.

From the perspective of effects, the question of employment of drones is; do the tactical results (killing of intended targets and "collaterals") outweigh the second order effects and strategic backlash of their use? A key to mitigation of negative effects is the use of and with domestic forces—ideally enabled by SFA and BPC activities conducted in the Engagement Ring. With use of these domestic (and other international forces) the U.S. will continue to strengthen a partnership, increase foreign security capacity, and diminish terror and criminal capabilities. Working with and through foreign partners has already proven effective and should be a cornerstone of Interdiction Ring activities. "That is because a crucial element in the success of U.S. counterterrorism has been the

---

[22] Cronin, *Why Drones Fail.*

close collaboration with allies on issues of terrorist financing, the extradition of terrorist suspects, and, most important, the sharing of vital intelligence."[23]

Terror and illicit criminal groups will also have their financial assets targeted. By definition, this is an Interdiction Ring effort, although it will be a continuous effort. Further demonstrating the link between activities and rings, financial targeting will benefit through the capture of illicit agents and the subsequent information and intelligence collection. The impact of financial targeting and interdiction cannot be over-stated. In the case of TOCs, their primary purpose is financial. With Hezbollah, funds are critical enabling aspects to their operations. Reduction of Hezbollah's and TOC's financial resources will have a corresponding effect on their political, paramilitary, information/media and social projects; reduction of means results in reduction of capability. Reduction of Hezbollah's social and media programs will lead to a corresponding compromise in Hezbollah's messaging to the people of Lebanon. This will provide greater opportunity for other agents, such as the Government of Lebanon or other international partners, to influence the Lebanese population.

Providing such an opportunity to influence is exactly the intent and design of Engagement Ring activities. This exhibits the critical nature of a coordinated relationship between the rings of the strategy. Financial interdiction and DA missions should also integrate into the broader approach with specific consideration of second order effects. There is no doubt that DA can have a great effect upon illicit groups by killing leaders and facilitators. Capturing them can have an even greater effect as they could be of significant intelligence value, enabling follow-on operations. However, DA is not an end in itself. "You can kill or capture enemy leaders. You can set back their organization.

---

[23] *Ibid.*

But I found that those kinds of blows were never decisive. The problem is, they give you the illusion of activity and the illusion of progress. In reality, terrorism is a symptom of wider problems."[24] Direct action, like financial interdiction, can be effective in preventing imminent or future attacks or efforts and degrading capabilities, but should also be viewed through the lens of providing operational space and opportunity for other efforts—particularly ones that will enable address of causal issues.

Interception Ring

The Interception Ring represents the "last line of defense" against a terror attack. This element of the approach also includes activity against TOC groups. The concerns, however, between the two groups necessarily take on different degrees of attention. With TOC groups, interception efforts are continuous status quo activities, which generally fall within the purview of law enforcement agencies within the United States and our Allies. With terror activities, the concerns are greater. The terror threat also brings other agencies into the forefront, such as the military and intelligence agencies.

Interception activities take place on both U.S. territory and in international spaces. This ring is the most geographic of the three rings as its focal point is the prevention of illicit activity on U.S. soil. Although focused on protecting the U.S., many efforts within this ring will take place in nations and space immediately adjacent to the U.S., in Mexico and Central America, Canada, and the Atlantic and Pacific Oceans.

As one would expect, many of the primary considerations of international law in the Engagement and Interdiction Rings do not apply to domestic actions. Although

---

[24] Stanley McChrystal, GEN, USA (Ret), interview by *Foreign Affairs*, Edited by Gideon Rose, New York: Lynda Hammes, (November/December 2013).

domestic law becomes a primary element in Interception Ring activities—such as law concerning posse comitatus, privacy, and individual rights—international law obviously still comes into play when taking action in neighboring states or in the international commons of the Atlantic and Pacific. Furthermore, if domestic actions are well coordinated within the broader context of the approach, there will be need to consider how domestic actions relate to follow-on actions where international law is applicable. Transitioning to follow-on actions again illustrates how engagement activities are critical to success. As engagement activities take place, both capabilities and *relationships* are developed. These relationships, between the U.S. and neighboring nations, are critical in facilitating successful interception (as well as interdiction) of terror and criminal agents.

A key point to this relationship is the ability to extradite criminals and terrorists from foreign nations to the United States for prosecution. This is critical in early stages of engagement as host states often lack effective judicial systems—due to compromise by TOC and terror groups. As foreign security, governance, and judicial capabilities mature, local governments will then be able to handle illicit agents themselves. Until then, illicit actors need to have fear of accountability. International relationships that provide for extradition to the United States can provide that fear of accountability. As before, the successful campaign against the Colombian cartels is instructive, "…extradition is vital. Trial and imprisonment in the United States was the only thing that the Colombian drug traffickers truly feared."[25]

Countering the nexus of Hezbollah and TOCs will require a comprehensive, multiagency, and multinational effort. The dynamic nature of Hezbollah and their TOC partners necessitates and equally dynamic approach to dismantle and destroy them. Most

---

[25] Bonner, *The New Cocaine Cowboys.*

significant in this effort are the indirect and non-violent efforts, which address root causes and go against sources of strength, reducing the operational freedom and reach of these organizations. Other actions, such as direct or financial action, can provide windows of opportunity, through gathering of information and intelligence or disrupting operations. Aggressive exploitation of these opportunities is paramount in order to remove the ungoverned spaces and associated populations that both Hezbollah and TOCs use as their operating foundations.

CHAPTER 6: CONCLUSION

Beyond its recent success and growth in the Levant, Hezbollah also maintains a strong presence in Central and South America. This presence has helped facilitate a nexus between Hezbollah and TOCs, particularly in Central America where Mexican Cartels and regional gangs have gained control over large portions of El Salvador, Guatemala, and Honduras. With these cartels and gangs comes trafficking expertise, specifically into the United States. This relationship between TOCs and Hezbollah should cause great concern to the U.S. The Hezbollah-cartel/gang nexus presents a unique threat to the United States largely due to the, "…porous southern border of the United States and abutting Mexico will be increasingly under the sway of hostile TOC groups, some of whom are closely aligned with state actors such as Venezuela and Iran that are overtly antagonistic to U.S. interests and goals."[1] This relationship takes on even greater importance when factoring in Iran's nuclear aspirations, with all of its attendant dynamics. "Further, the standoff with Iran over its nuclear program, and the uncertainty of whether Israel might attack Iran drawing the United States into a confrontation, only heightens concern that Iran or its agents would attempt to exploit the porous Southwest border for retaliation."[2]

Due to the advanced development and capability of Hezbollah, many have concluded that its leadership will avoid direct involvement in an attack against U.S. soil. While this perspective bears merit, Hezbollah's capability provides it with options such

---

[1] Douglass Farah, *Transnational Organized Crime, Terrorism, and Criminalized States in Latin America: An Emerging Tier-One National Security Priority.* (Carlisle Barracks, PA: U.S. Army War College Strategic Studies Institute, 2012): 90.
[2] Rep. Michael T. McCaul, *A Line in the Sand: Countering Crime, Violence and Terror at the Southwest Border.* (Washington, D.C.: U.S. House of Representatives, House Committee on Homeland Security, 2012): 3.

as the use of a proxy or other indirect approaches to attack the United States. Gangs and cartels may provide just such vehicles. As seen with the recent assassination attempt against the Saudi Ambassador to the United States, Iran's agents (which Hezbollah is a primary member) have demonstrated a willingness to take action within the United States. Compounding this concern is the willingness of TOC agents, as was seen in the Zeta's role in the assassination attempt, to serve as the terminal actors in acts of terror in the United States.

The global reach of Hezbollah and TOCs illustrate a vast capability, which expands the threat aperture. "Latin American networks now extend not only to the United States and Canada, but outward to Sub-Saharan Africa, Europe, and Asia, where they have begun to form alliances with other networks."[3] This reach offers great functionality for all concerned, whether for criminal or terrorist activity, or both.

In the face of the threat presented by a functional relationship between Hezbollah and TOCs, the United States should develop an approach that not only recognizes this nexus, but also sees these organizations, and those like them, as similar. In such an approach, the primary focus should be upon addressing the root causes and factors and strengths of these groups, rather than a focus upon elimination of leadership. The first element of the approach should be to *Engage* the host nation and international community as a whole in order to develop a common understanding of the threat and develop international legal consensus for action. With this consensus, U.S. and international efforts can begin to address the causal factors that enable Hezbollah and TOCs to operate freely and effectively. Critical to this effort is an effort to build the capability and capacity of local governments to confront these illicit groups while also

[3] Farah, *Transnational Organized Crime*, 3.

building and preserving their legitimacy with their domestic populations. Once the governments of these nations act as primary guarantor of security and services, with the illicit group(s) discredited and considered illegitimate (or apostate), the effort will have passed the "tipping point" of the struggle.

A methodology designed to combat the threat presented by a nexus of Hezbollah and TOCs must have its focus and preponderance of effort outside of the United States. This is because not only it is desirable to engage this threat outside the U.S., but more significantly, any lasting and effective effort to defeat this concern must address the root causes and base elements. Furthermore, the primary mechanism of success will not be U.S. actions themselves, but rather the actions of our international partners. This relationship is critical to success in this endeavor, for both the U.S. and our current and potential partners.

While terrorism and TOCs are a great concern of the United States, even in the face of a WMD attack, they are not existential. In other nations, such as Lebanon, Mexico, and those of the Northern Triangle, the threat posed by Hezbollah and TOCs is grave, and could lead to state failure. The existence of the narco-state then, in turn, presents a threat to the United States and other stable nations, as well as to the entire international system. "By seeking to embed themselves irrevocably in a country's political system and win exclusive control over a segment of the population, mezzanine rulers jeopardize domestic stability. When they resort to terrorism, piracy, insurgency, or other means to advance ideological, ethnic, or nationalist agendas, they pose a threat that goes well beyond the borders of the host state."[4]

---

[4] Jami Miscik & Michael Crawford, "The Rise of the Mezzanine Rulers: The New Frontier for International Law." Edited by Jr James F. Hoge. *Foreign Affairs* 89, no. 6 (November/December 2010): 123.

The primary utility of U.S. actions will be as enablers to our partners. These enabling actions come primarily in the form of support and development activities that help a nation to gain and/or maintain capability and legitimacy, in the face of illicit actors such as Hezbollah and TOC groups. Direct action, when appropriate is another enabling activity that gains the host nation and other international actors opportunity—either to inject a developing capability or to hold off or reduce the threat for a period. As a point of emphasis, it is important to note that DA is rarely an end in itself, but rather a supporting component of a larger approach.

Getting to the "tipping point" will require significant *Interdiction* and *Interception* efforts, both in prevention of imminent attacks, but more significantly in disrupting the activities of illicit groups and killing and capturing key leaders and operatives. These actions will enable information collection and intelligence generation that can lead to further DA operations while presenting opportunities for the introduction of *Engagement* efforts, and time for them to take effect with target populations.

For an approach of this nature to work, it will require firm direction from the Chief Executive, along with vigilant supervision, specifically to ensure that effective multi-agency coordination and integration is taking place. This multi-agency approach is critical, requiring vigilant supervision, due to the tendency of agencies to act myopically, potentially losing sight of broader implications of isolated actions.

This proposed approach, with all of its attendant elements, while centered upon Hezbollah and Central American TOCs, supports a wider purpose. The recent growth and success of these groups should serve as both an immediate concern and a long-term warning to the United States and the West. "Any single one of these movements can be dismissed as anomalous, but taken collectively as a phenomenon, they represent a unique long-term challenge to governments, Western policymakers, and the precepts of international law."[5] Particularly in the case of Hezbollah, there is strong likelihood that others will emulate their organizational model. Although there has been success against terror and TOC organizations in recent history, such as the case with the Colombian drug cartels, the Westphalian world has yet to effectively recognize, let alone deal with and eliminate, a non-state group with the breadth and capability of Hezbollah. In building the national and international capacity to destroy or make irrelevant a non-state, terror, political, social, media/information and criminal group such as Hezbollah, the U.S. and international community will go far in facing emergent challenges of the 21st Century.

---

[5] Miscik & Crawford, *The Rise of the Mezzanine Rulers*, 123.

BIBLIOGRAPHY

Aboul-Enein, Youssef H. *Militant Islamist Ideology: Understanding the Global Threat.* Annapolis, Marlyland: Naval Institute Press, 2010.

Alexander Hamilton, John Jay, and James Madison. *The Federalist Papers.* Metairie, LA: Megalodon Entertainment LLC, 2010.

Azani, Eitan. *Hezbollah: The Story of the party of God.* New York: Palgrave MacMillan, 2009.

Azani, Etan, Congressman Dana Rohrabacher, & Urbancic, Franck C. "Hezbollah's Global reach." *Hearing of the House Committee on International Relations-- Subcommittee on International Terrorism and Nonproliferation.* Washington, D.C., September 2006.

Biettel, Sullivan. *Latin America: Terrorism Issues.* Washington D.C.: Congressional Research Service, 2013.

Blanford, Nicholas. "Terrorism and Insurgency: Deconstructing Hizbullah's Surprise Military Prowess." *Jane's Intelligence Review* 18, no. 11 (November 2006): 20-27.

Bonner, Robert C. "The New Cocaine Cowboys: How to Defeat Mexico's Drug Cartels." Edited by JR James F. Hoge. *Foreign Affairs* (David Kellogg) 89, no. 4 (July/August 2010): 35-47.

Boot, Max. *Invisible Armies: An Epic History of Guerrilla Warfare from Ancient Times to the Present.* New York & London: Liveright Publishing Corporation, 2013.

Brice, Arthur. "Iran, Hezbollah mine Latin America for revenue, recruits, analysts say." *cnn.com.* June 3, 2013. http://www.cnn.com/2013/06/03/world/americas/iran-latin-america/index.html (accessed October 1, 2013).

Burns, WIlliam J. *www.state.gov/p/us/rm/2011/169045.htm#.* July 25, 2011. (accessed January 3, 2014).

Carter, Sara A. "Exclusive: Hezbollah uses Mexican drug routes into U.S." *Washington Times,* March 27, 2009.

CATO Institute. *The Weaponization of Immigration.* Washington, D.C.: Center for Imigration Studies, 2008.

U.S. Congress, House Committee on Homeland Security. *Iran, Hezbollah, and the Threat to the Homeland.* 112th Congress, March 21, 2012.

National Security Council. "Strategy to Combat Transnational Organized Crime: Addressing Converging Threats to National Security." Washington, D.C., 2011.

Cronin, Audrey Kurth. "Why Drones Fail: When Tactics Drive Strategy." Edited by Gideon Rose. *Foreign Affairs* (Lynda Hammes) 92, no. 4 (July/August 2013): 44-54.

Department, Treasury. *www.treasury.gov/resource-center/terrorist-illicit-finance/pages/default.aspx.* (accessed January 3, 2014).

Dettmer, Jamie. "MS-13 and Calle 18 Developing Strong Relationships with Drug Cartels." *Dialogo*, December 19, 2011.

Division, Federal Research. *Terrorist and Organized Crime Groups in the Tri-Border Area.* Washington, D.C.: Library of Congress, 2003.

Enos, Olivia. *Crime-Ridden Mexican Border Fosters Human Trafficking.* August 11, 2011. http://blog.heritage.org/2011/08/11/crime-ridden-mexican-border-fosters-human-trafficking/ (accessed November 25, 2013).

Espach, Ralph & Asfura-Heim, Patricio. "The Rise of Mexico's Self-Defense Forces: Vigilante Justice South of the Border." Edited by Gideon Rose. *Foreign Affairs* (Lynda Hammes) 92, no. 4 (July/August 2013): 143-150.

Farah, Douglas. "Central America's Northern Triangle: A Time for turmoil and Transitions." *Prism* (Center for Complex Operations) 4, no. 3 (2013): 88-109.

—. *Transnational Organized Crime, Terrorism, and Criminalized States in Latin America: An Emerging Tier-One National Security Priority.* Carlisle Barracks, PA: U.S. Army War College Strategic Studies Institute, 2012.

Gertz, Bill. *Hizbullah building terror infrastructure in U.S., infiltrating from Mexico.* June 10, 2010. http://worldtribune.com/worldtribune/WTARC/2010/ss_terror0516_06_11.asp (accessed November 25, 2013).

Glenn, Russell W. *All Glory is Fleeting.* Santa Monica, CA: RAND Corporation, 2012.

Human trafficking in Mexico targets women and children. January 2013, 2010. http://www.cnn.com/2010/WORLD/americas/01/13/mexico.human.traffic.drug/index.html (accessed November 25, 2013).

Jaber, Hala. *Hezbollah, Born with a Vengeance.* New York: Columbia University Press, 1997.

Kyl, John, Feith, Douglas J. Feith, & Fonte, John. "The War of Law: How New International Law Undermines Democratic Sovereignty." Edited by Gideon Rose. *Foreign Affairs* (Lynda Hammes) 92, no. 4 (July/August 2013): 115-125.

Jorisch, Avi. *Beacon of Hatred: Inside Hizballah's Al-Manar Television.* Washington D.C.: Washington Institue for Near East Policy, 2004.

Kilcullen, David J. "The City as a System: Future Conflict and Urban Resistance." *The Fletcher Forum of World Affairs* 36, no. 2 (Summer 2012): 19-39.

Levitt, Matthew. *Hezbollah: Narco-Islamism.* Washington, D.C.: The Washington Institute for Near East Policy, 2009.

Malone, David M. & Berdal, Mats. *Greed & Grievance: Economic Agendas in Civil Wars.* Boulder, CO: Lynne Rienner Publishers, 2000.

Mauro, Ryan. *Growing Hezbollah Presence in Southwest U.S.* October 13, 2013. http://m.clarionproject.org/analysis/hezbollah-tattoos-increasing-found-us-prison-inmates (accessed February 11, 2014).

Mazzitelli, Antonio L. "The New Transatlantic Bonanza: Cocaine on Highway 10." Western Hemisphere Security Analysis Center, Florida International University, Miami, 2011.

McCaul, Rep. Michael T. *A Line in the Sand: Countering Crime, Violence and Terror at the Southwest Border.* Washington, D.C.: U.S. House of Representatives, House Committee on Homeland Security, 2012.

McChrystal, Stanley, GEN, USA (Ret), interview by Foreign Affairs, Edited by Gideon Rose. New York: Lynda Hammes, (Novemeber/December 2013).

Miryekta, Cyrus. "Hezbollah in the Tri-Border Area of South America." *smallwarsjournal.com.* (accessed October 1, 2013).

Miscik, Jami & Crawford, Michael. "The Rise of the Mezzanine Rulers: The New Frontier for International Law." Edited by Jr James F. Hoge. *Foreign Affairs* (David Kellogg) 89, no. 6 (November/December 2010): 123-132.

"National Counterterrorism Strategy." Washington D.C.: The White House, 2011.

Noriega, Roger F. *Hezbollah's strategic shift: A global terrorist threat.* March 20, 2013.

http://www.aei.org/speech/foreign-and-defense-policy/regional/middle-east-and-north-africa/hezbollahs-strategic-shift-a-global-terrorist-threat/ (accessed February 11, 2014).

Norton, Richard. *Amal and the Shi'a: Struggle for the Soul of Lebanon.* Austin: University of Texas Press, 1987.

—. *Hezbollah: A Short History.* Princeton: Princeton University Press, 2007.

National Security Council. *NSC.* http://www.whitehouse.gov/administration/eop/nsc/transnational-crime/definition (accessed January 22, 2014).

Patrick, Stewart. "The Unruled World: The Case for Good Enough Global Governance." Edited by Gideon Rose. *Foreign Affairs* (Lynda Hammes) 93, no. 1 (January/February 2014): 58-73.

Potter, Matt. *Outlaws Inc.: Under the Radar and on the Black Market with the World's Most Dangerous Smugglers.* New York: Bloomsbury, 2001.

"Press Release, U.S. Attourney's Office for the Southern District of New York." December 15, 2011.

Preston, Thomas & Herrmann, Margaret. "Presidents, Advisers, and Foreign Policy: The Effect of Leadership Style on Executive Arrangements." *Political Psychology* 15, no. 1 (1994): 75-95.

Schenker, David. "Shiites Against Hezbollah." *The Weekly Standard*, 2006.

Shelley, Louise. "The Unholy Trinity: Transnational Crime, Corruption, and Terrorism." *Brown Journal of World Affairs* XI, no. 2 (Winter/Spring 2005): 101-111.

Shultz, Richard & Godson , Roy. *Adapting America's Security Paradigm and Security Agenda.* Washington, D.C.: National Strategy Information Center, 2010.

State, Department of. *www.state.gov/j/ct/programs/index.htm#ctf.* (accessed 1 3, 2014).

Tung, Mao Tse. *On Guerrilla Warfare.* Urbana & Chicago: University of Illinois Press, 1961.

U.S. v. Manssor Arbabsiar and Gholam Shakuri. 1:11-cr-00897-JFK (U.S. District Court for the Southern District of New York).

Yarger, Harry R. *Strategic Theory for the 21st Century: The Little Book on Big Strategy.* Carlisle, PA: Strategic Studies Institute, U.S. Army, 2006.

VITA

LtCol Zeman was commissioned in 1993 through the Platoon Leaders Course. Upon designation as an infantry officer and completion of Infantry Officer's Course, then 2dLt Zeman reported for duty as a platoon commander in 2d Marine Division at Camp Lejeune, NC. Since then, LtCol Zeman has completed six deployments (three combat) and served in a variety of operational billets including Force Reconnaissance Detachment Commander for the 24th Marine Expeditionary Unit, Assistant Operations Officer for 7th Marines (OIF 2), and the Battalion Executive Officer for 3d Battalion, 4th Marines (OIF 3). His posting highlights include; Marine Officer Instructor at College of the Holy Cross, Strategic Analyst in the Strategic Initiatives Group at Headquarters, Marine Corps, Executive Officer & Operations Officer for the standup of the Afghan 215th Corps in Helmand, Afghanistan, and as Headquarters Battalion Commander and Plans Officer for the Marine Air Ground Task Force Training Center, Twentynine Palms, California. LtCol Zeman is a graduate of Boston University with a BA in History and holds a Master of Arts degree from the Fletcher School of Law and Diplomacy, Tufts University.